Granny's Cuss Words

Got a potty mouth? Need some safe
words to say around Granny? Or the kids?

Enjoy this assortment of PG-rated
coloring pages
while you relax and de-stress.

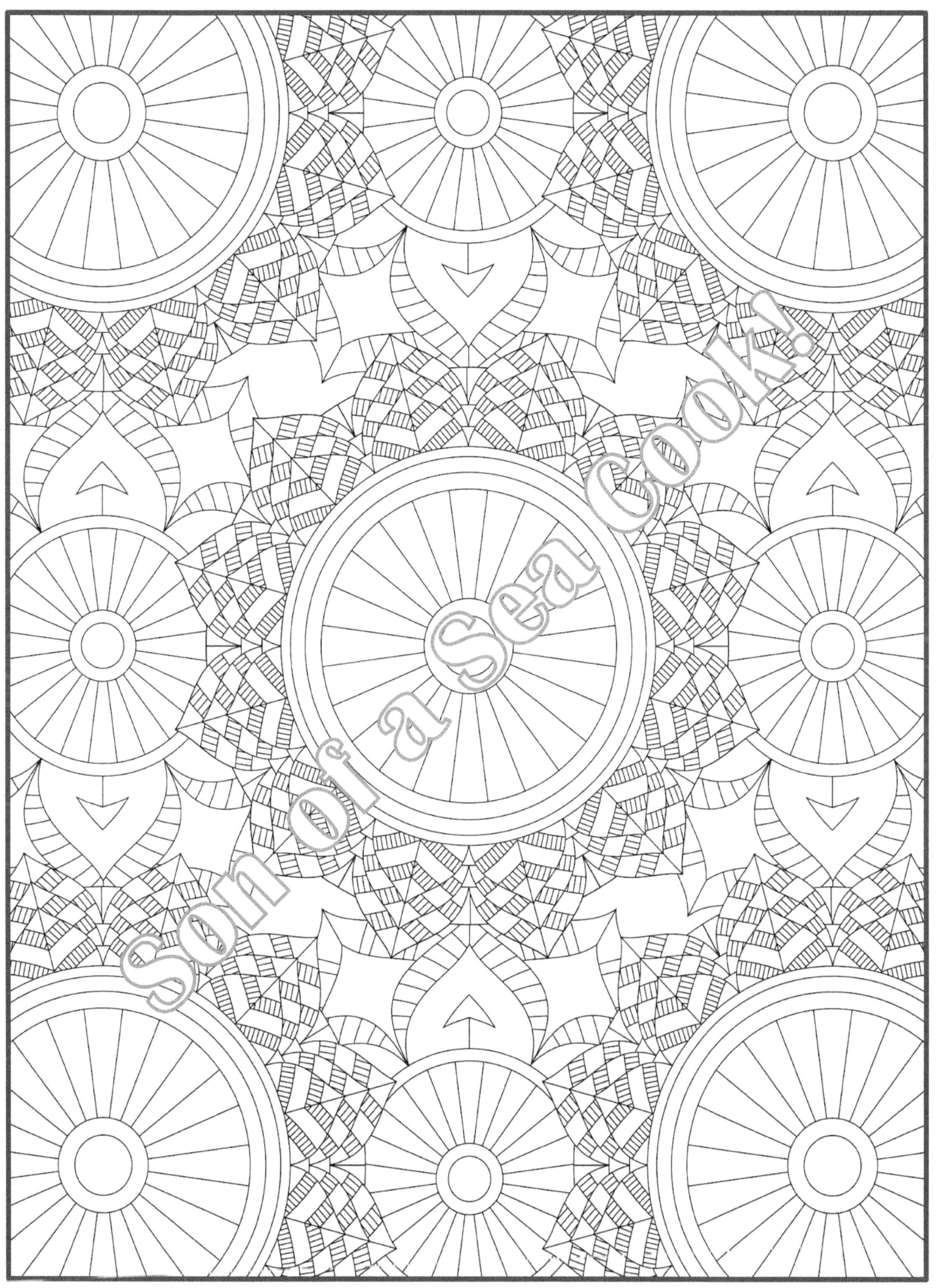

Page intentionally left blank for framing.

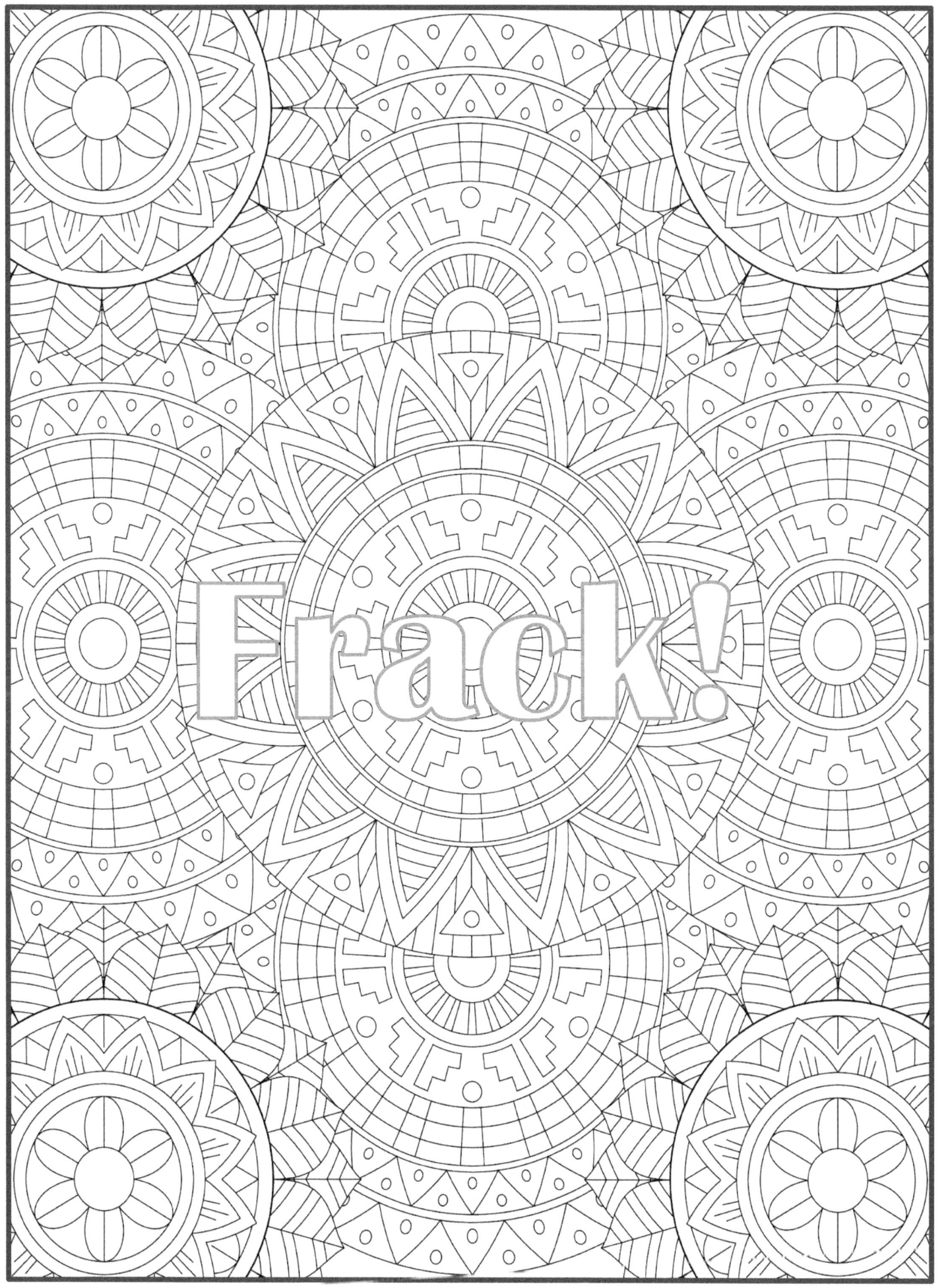

Page intentionally left blank for framing.

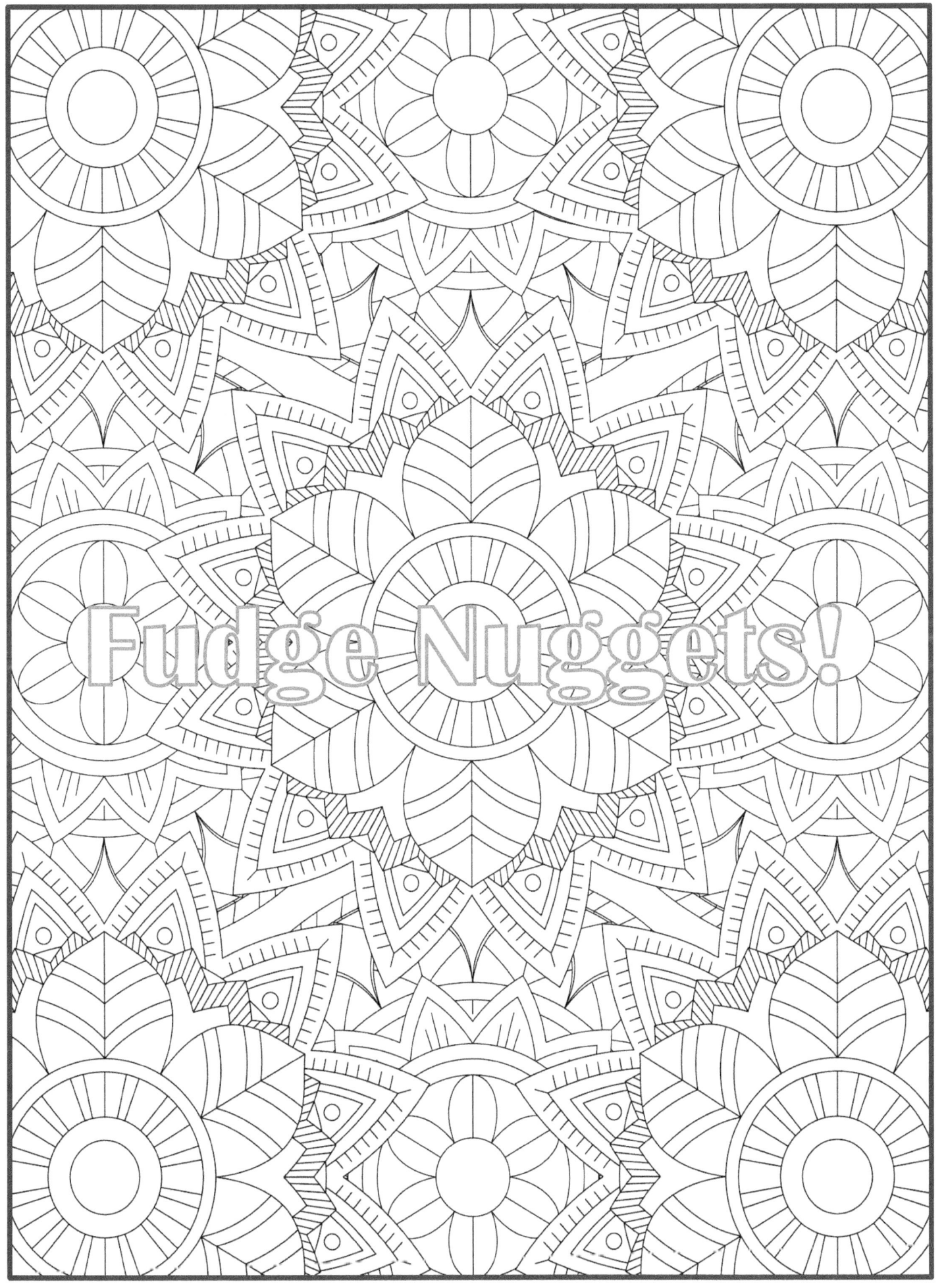

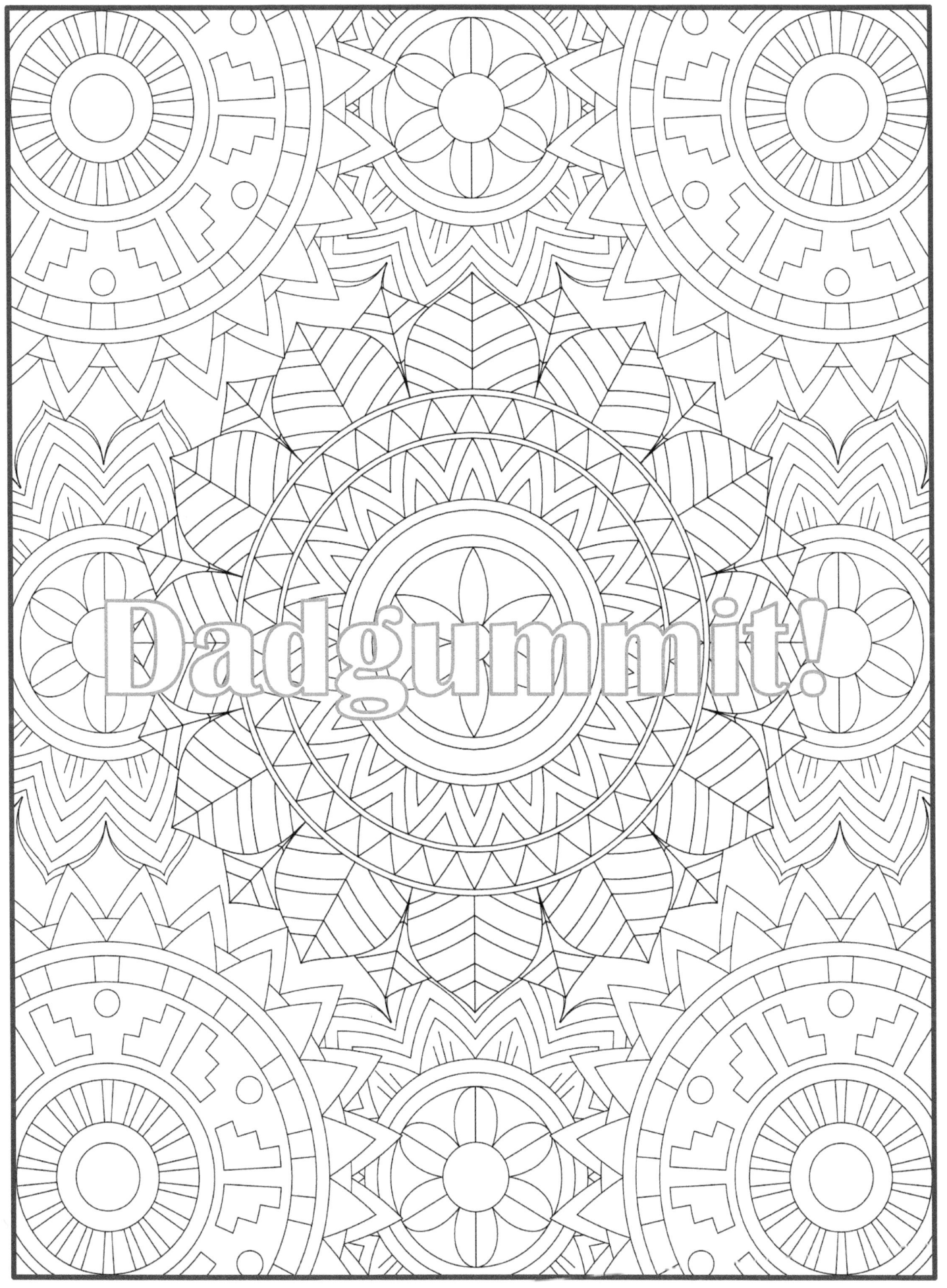

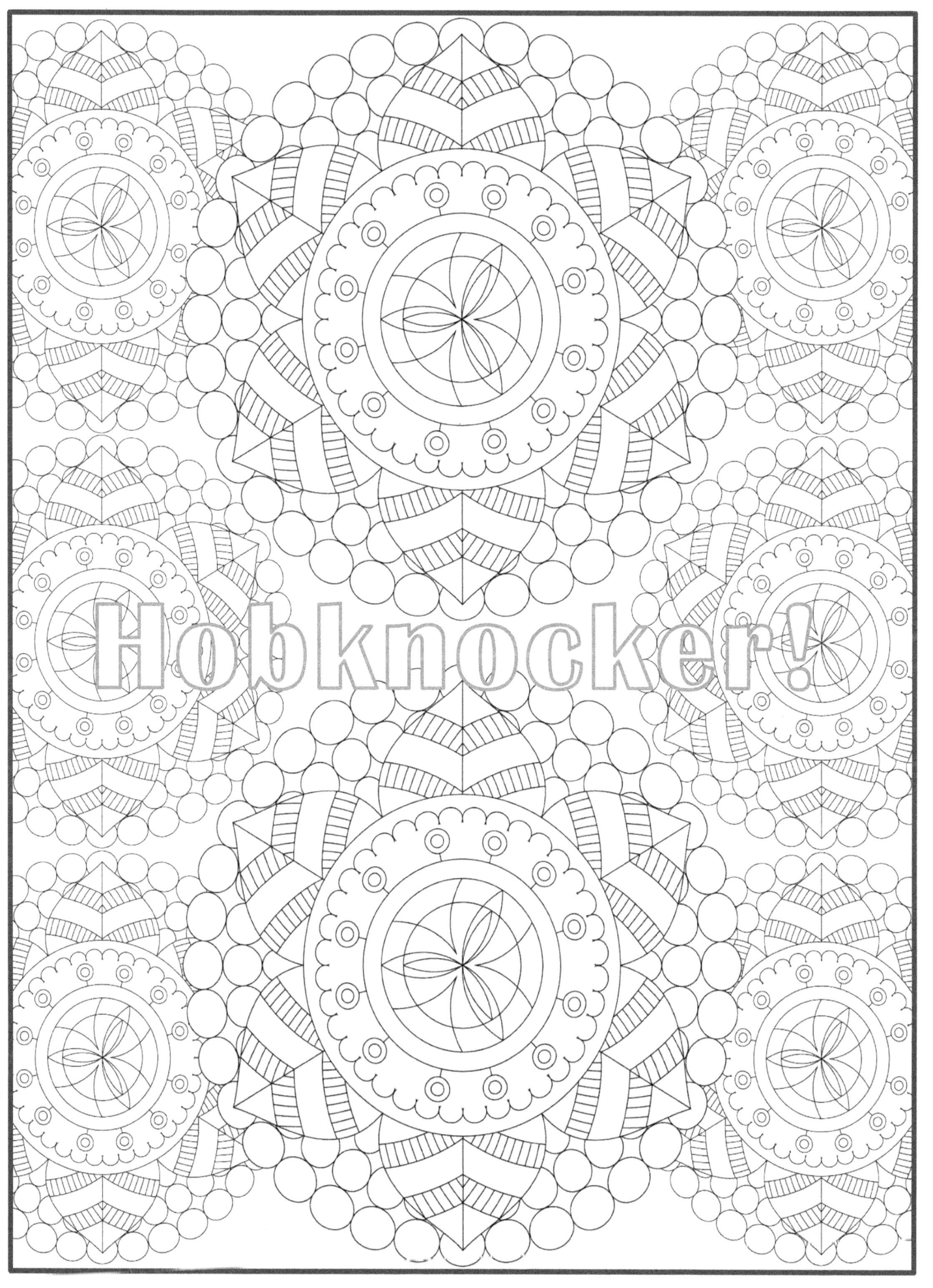

Page intentionally left blank for framing.

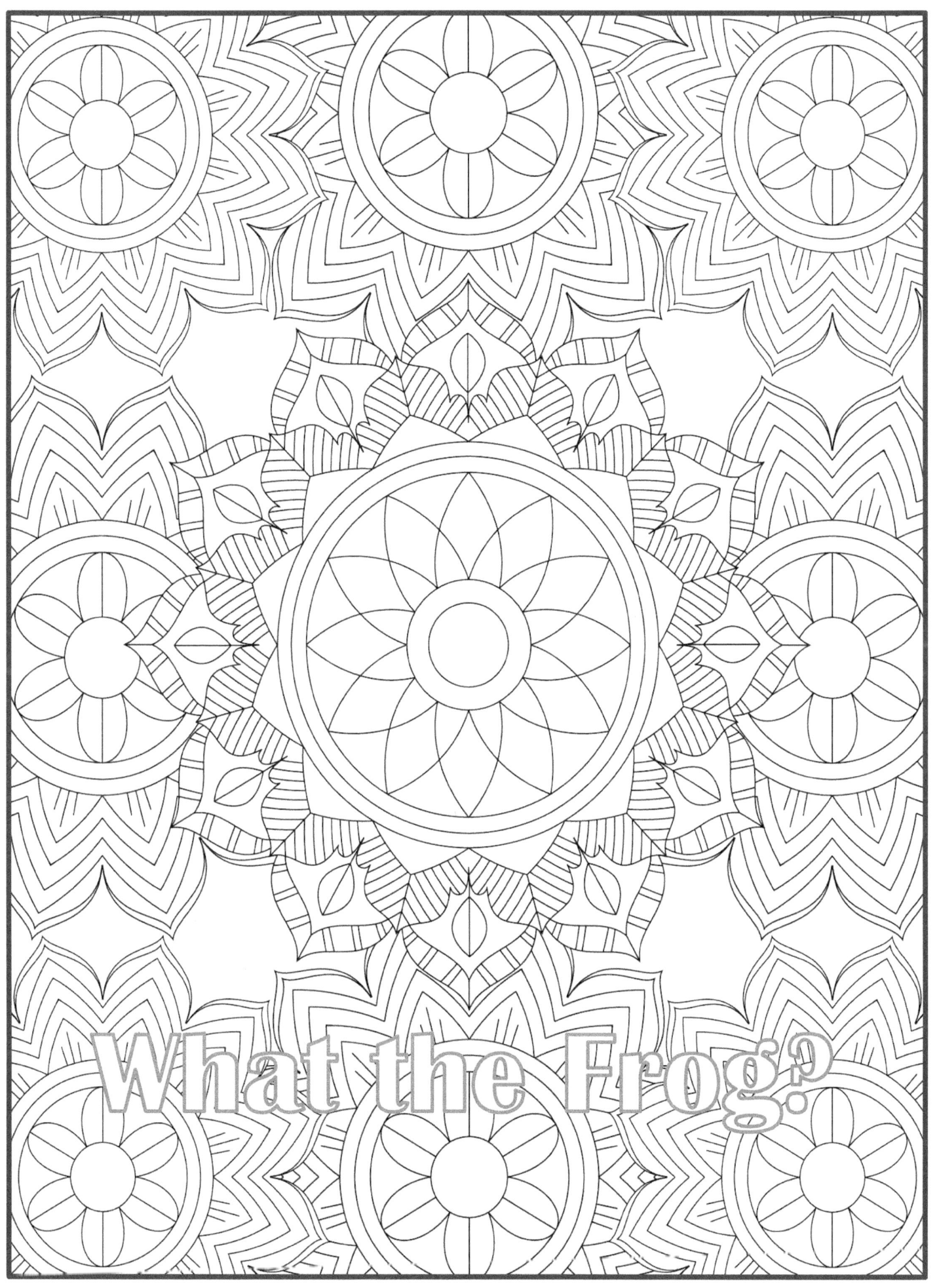

Page intentionally left blank for framing.

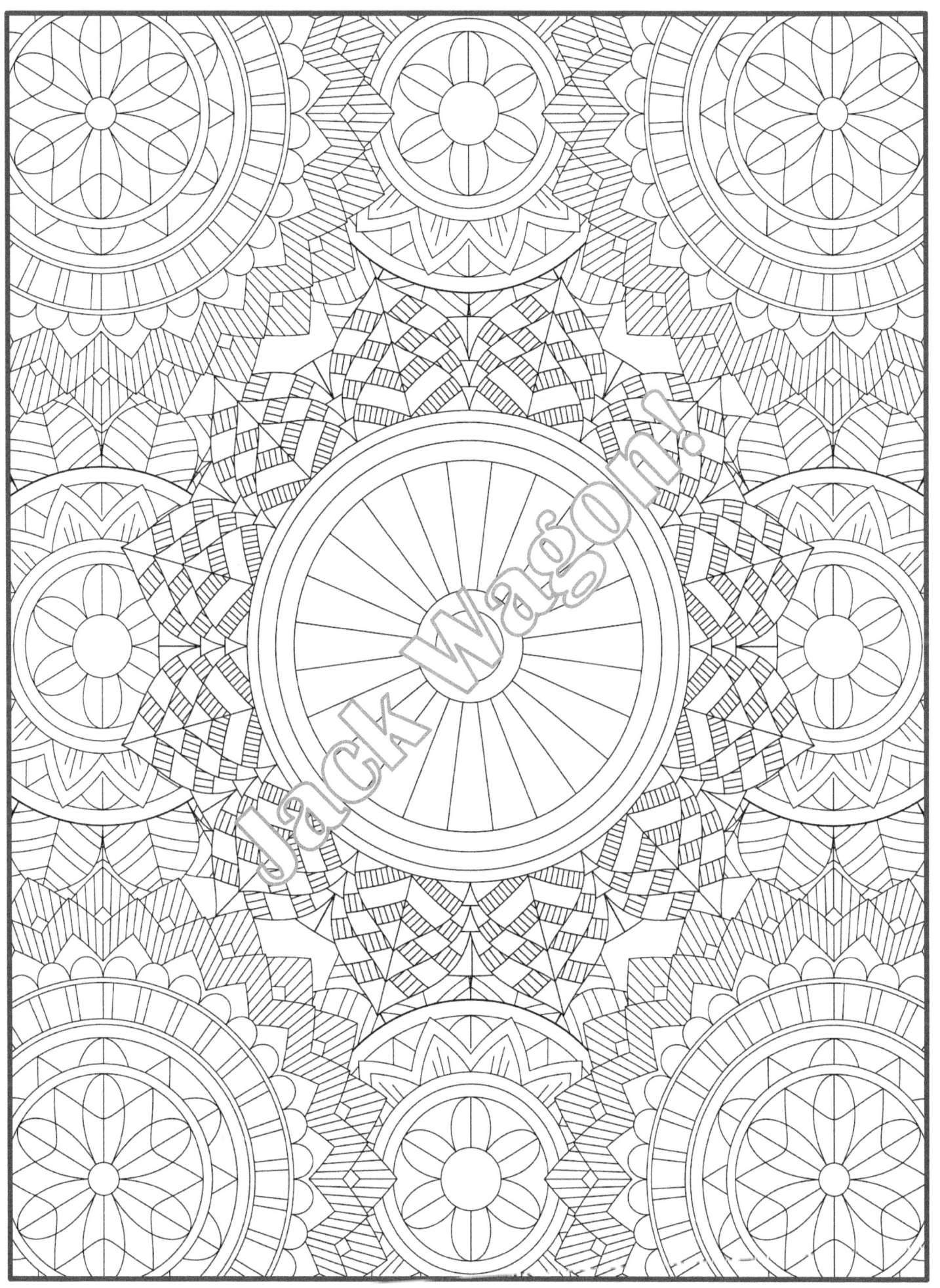

Page intentionally left blank for framing.

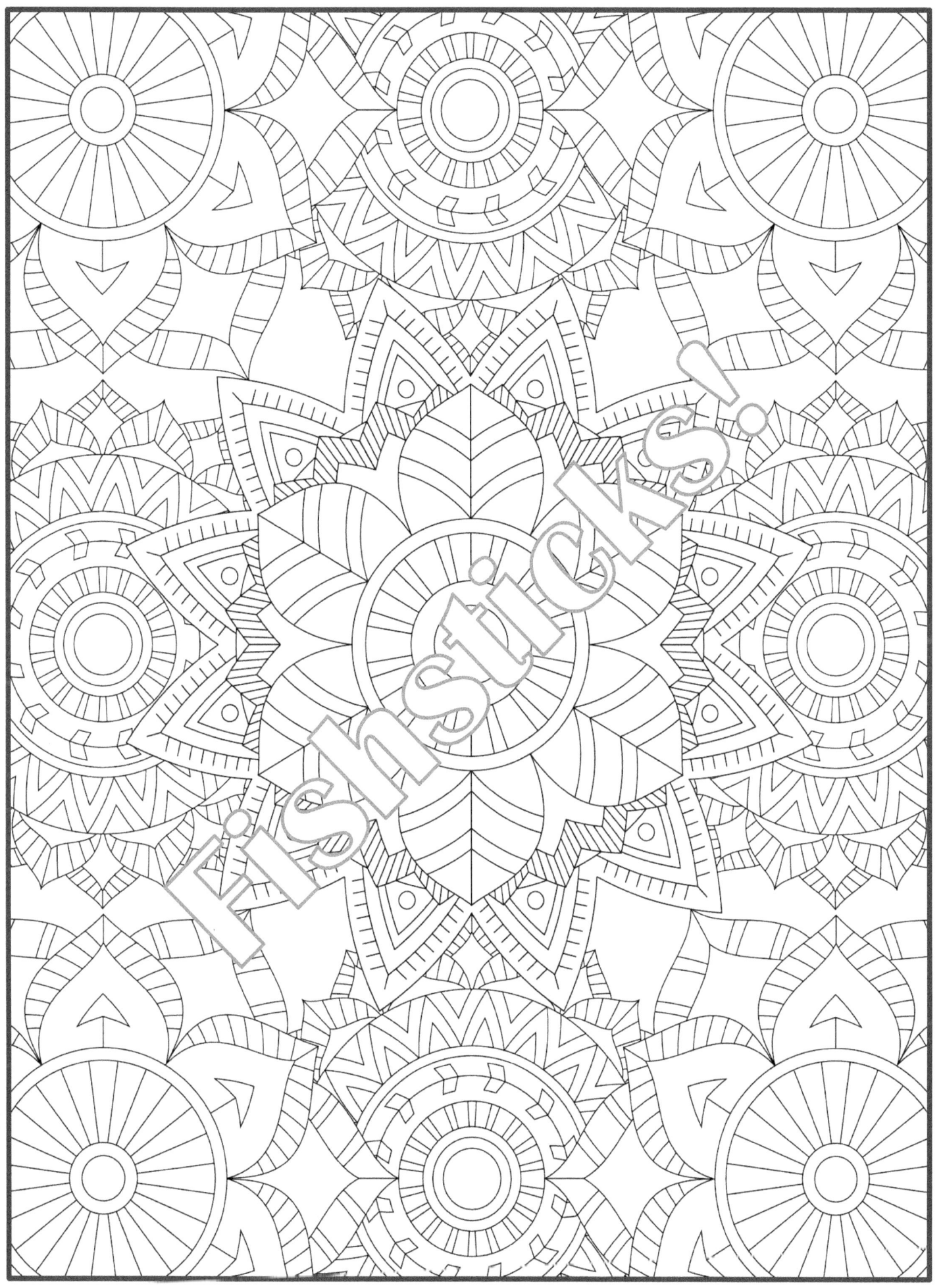

Page intentionally left blank for framing.

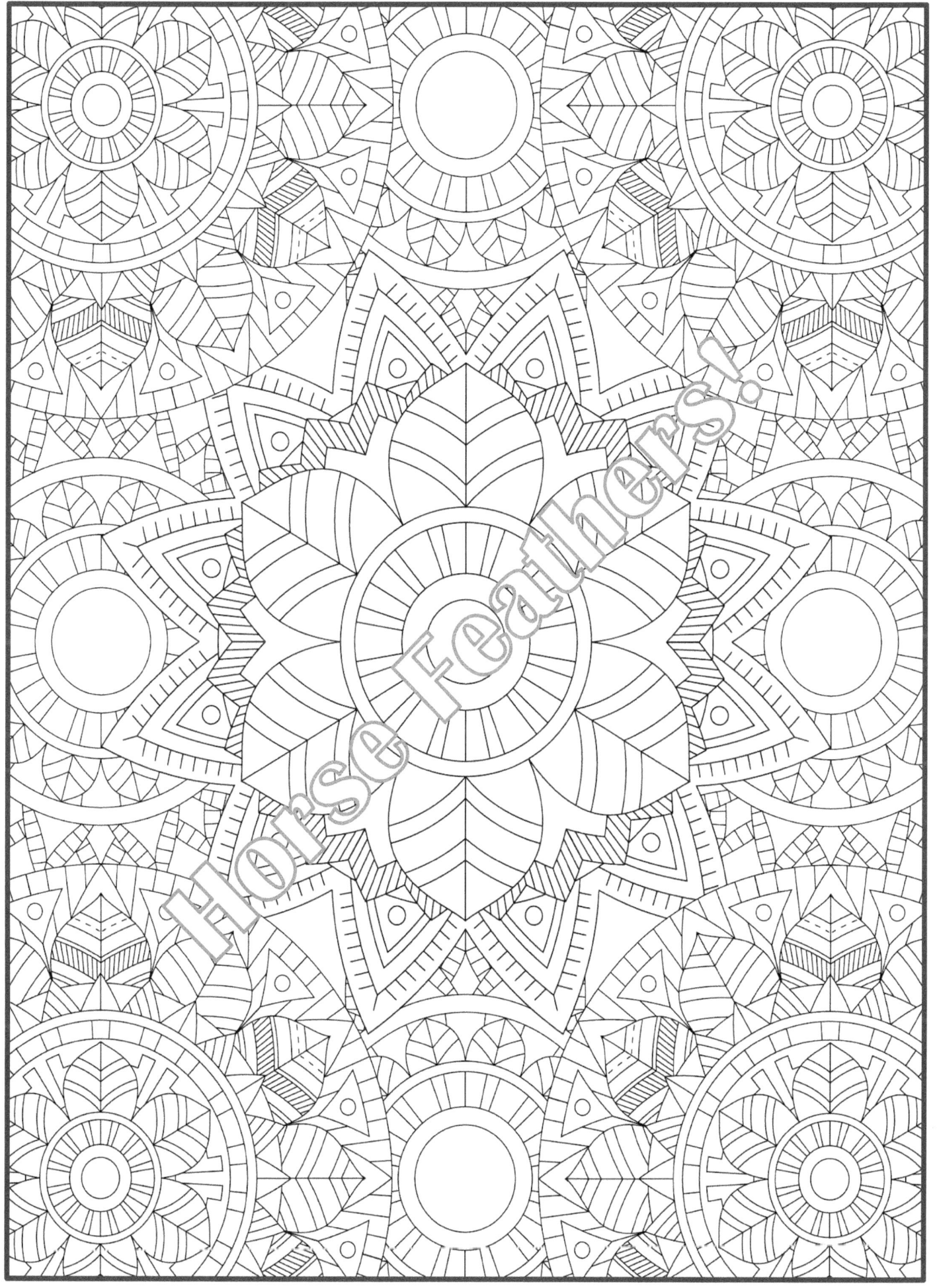

Page intentionally left blank for framing.

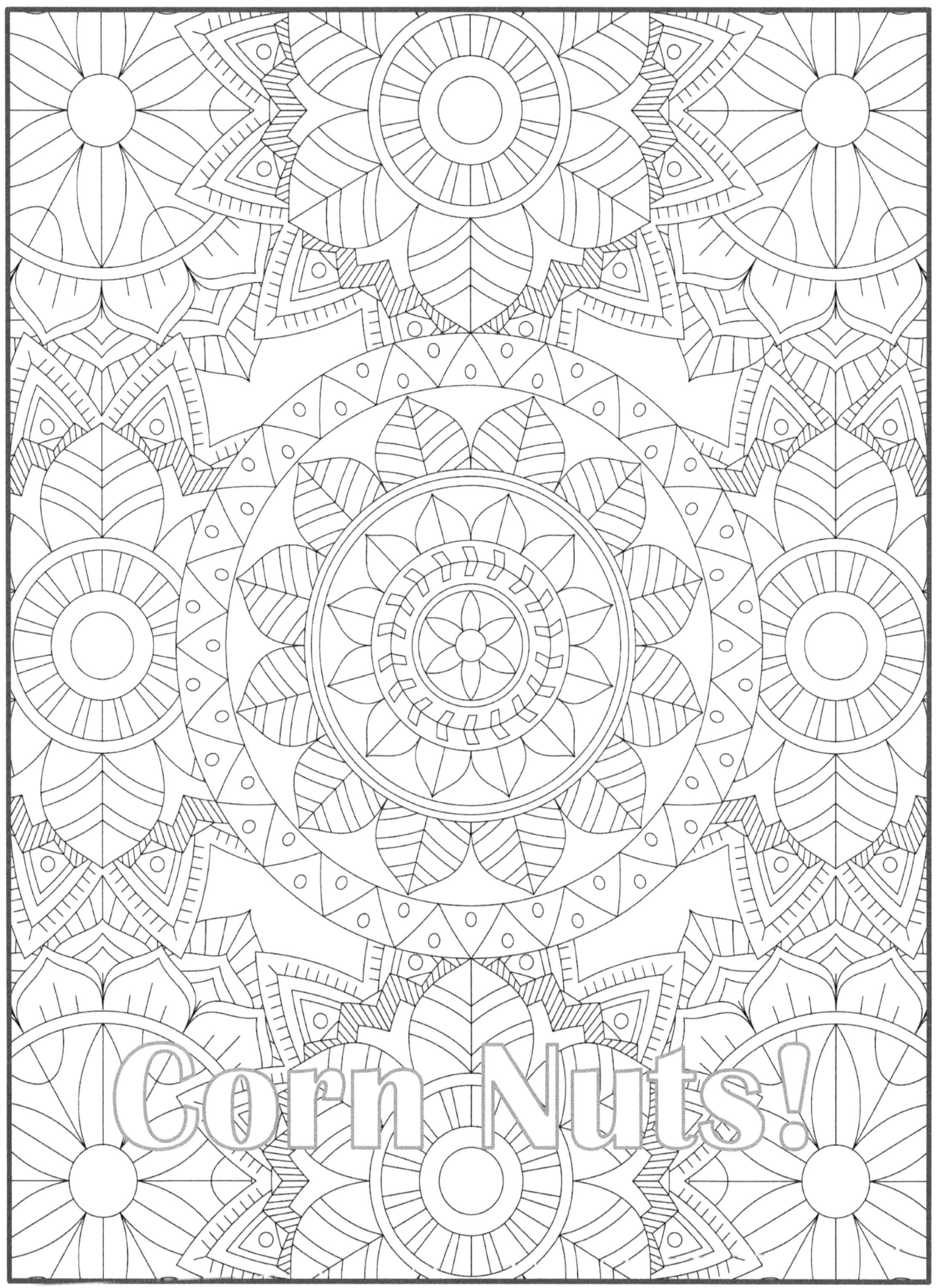

Page intentionally left blank for framing.

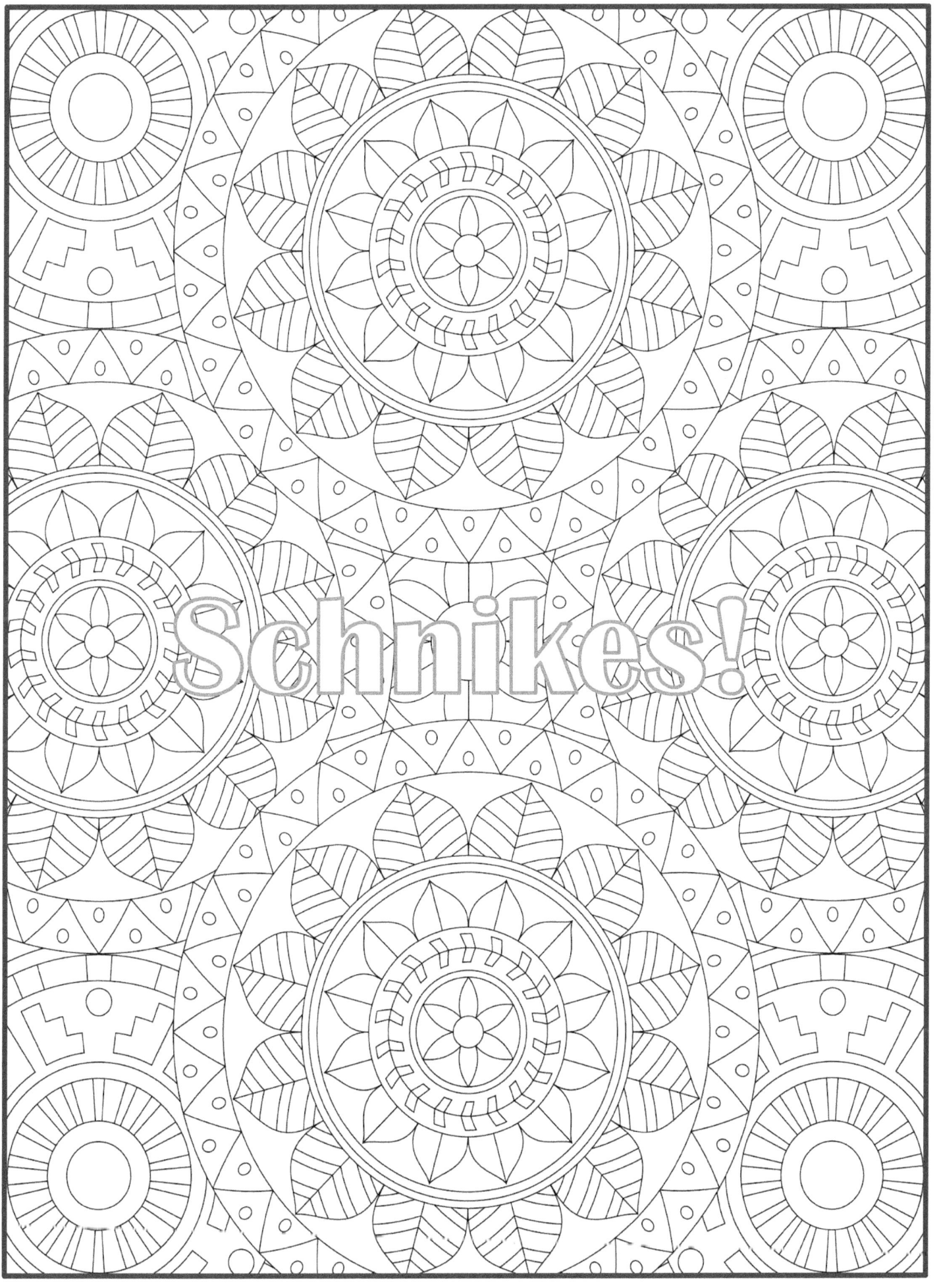

Page intentionally left blank for framing.

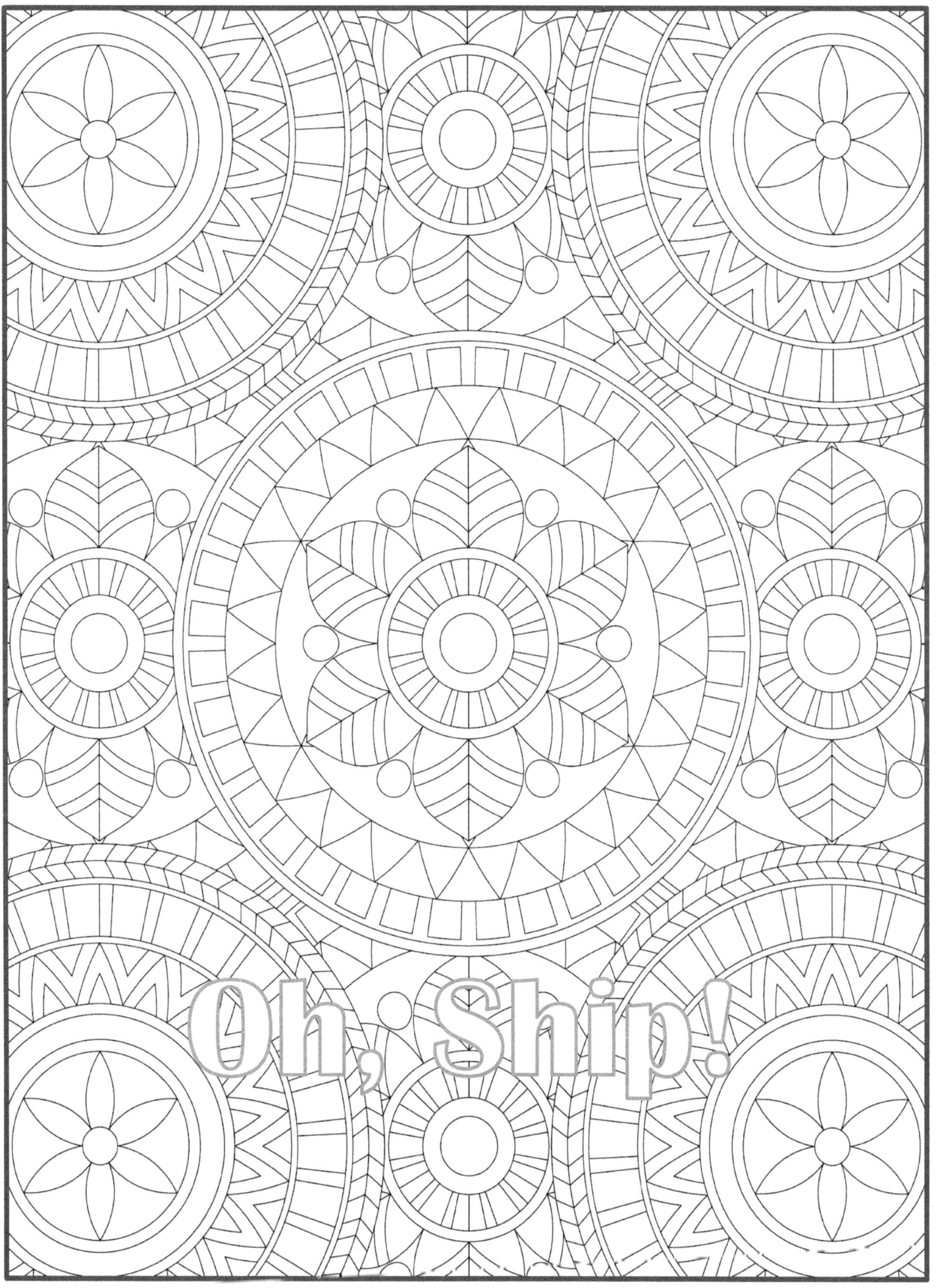

Page intentionally left blank for framing.

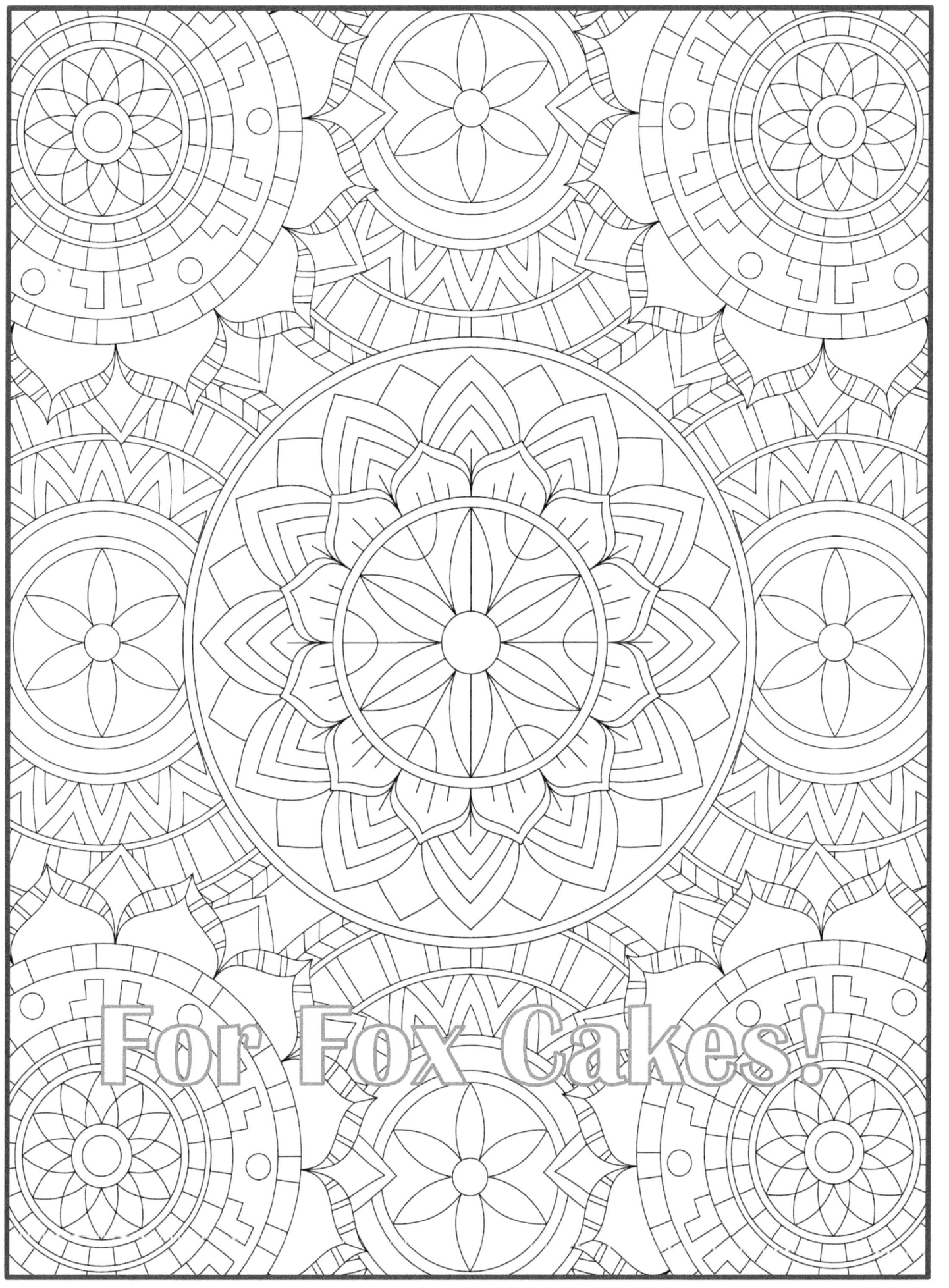

For Fox Cakes!

Page intentionally left blank for framing.

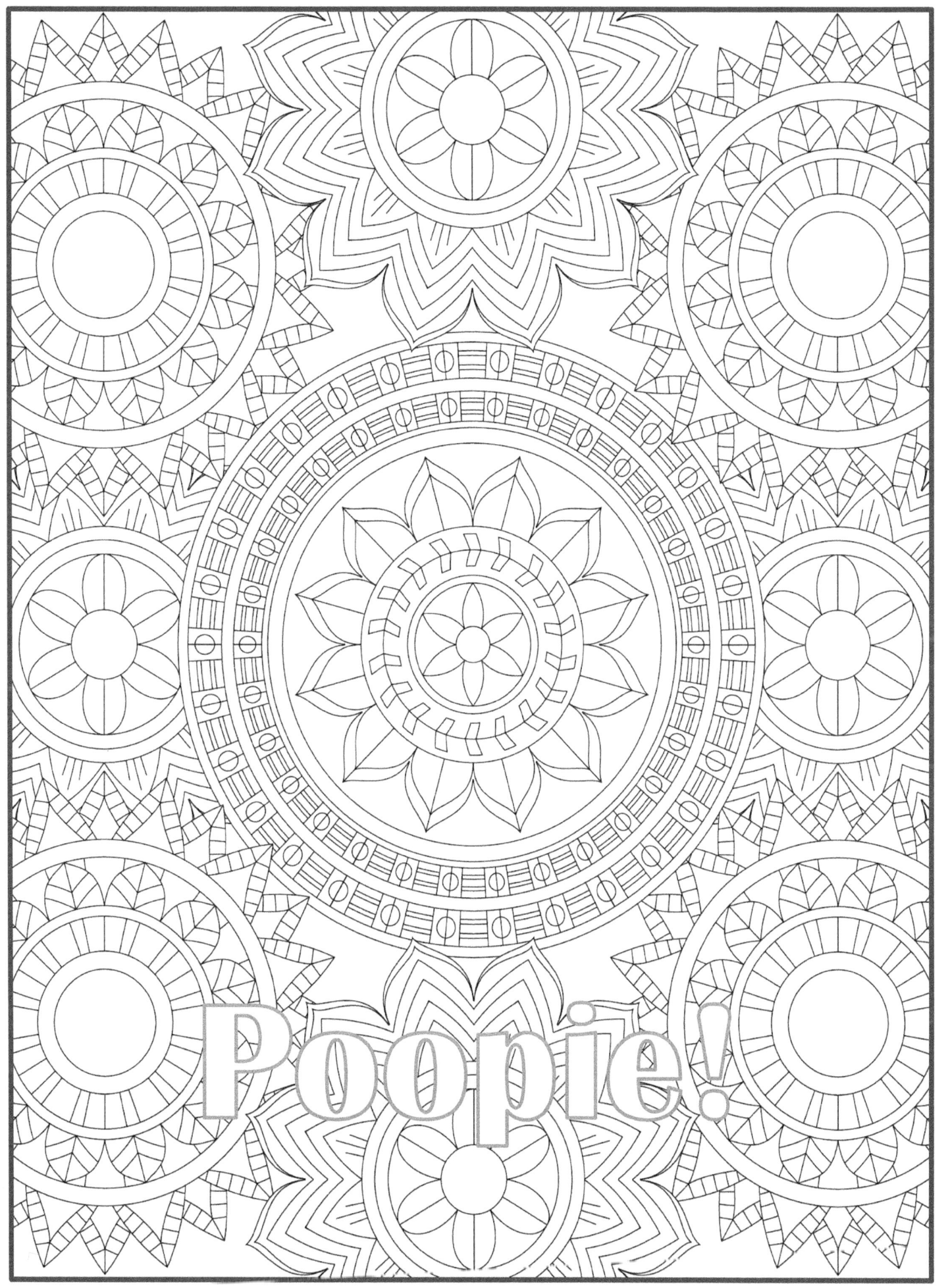

Page intentionally left blank for framing.

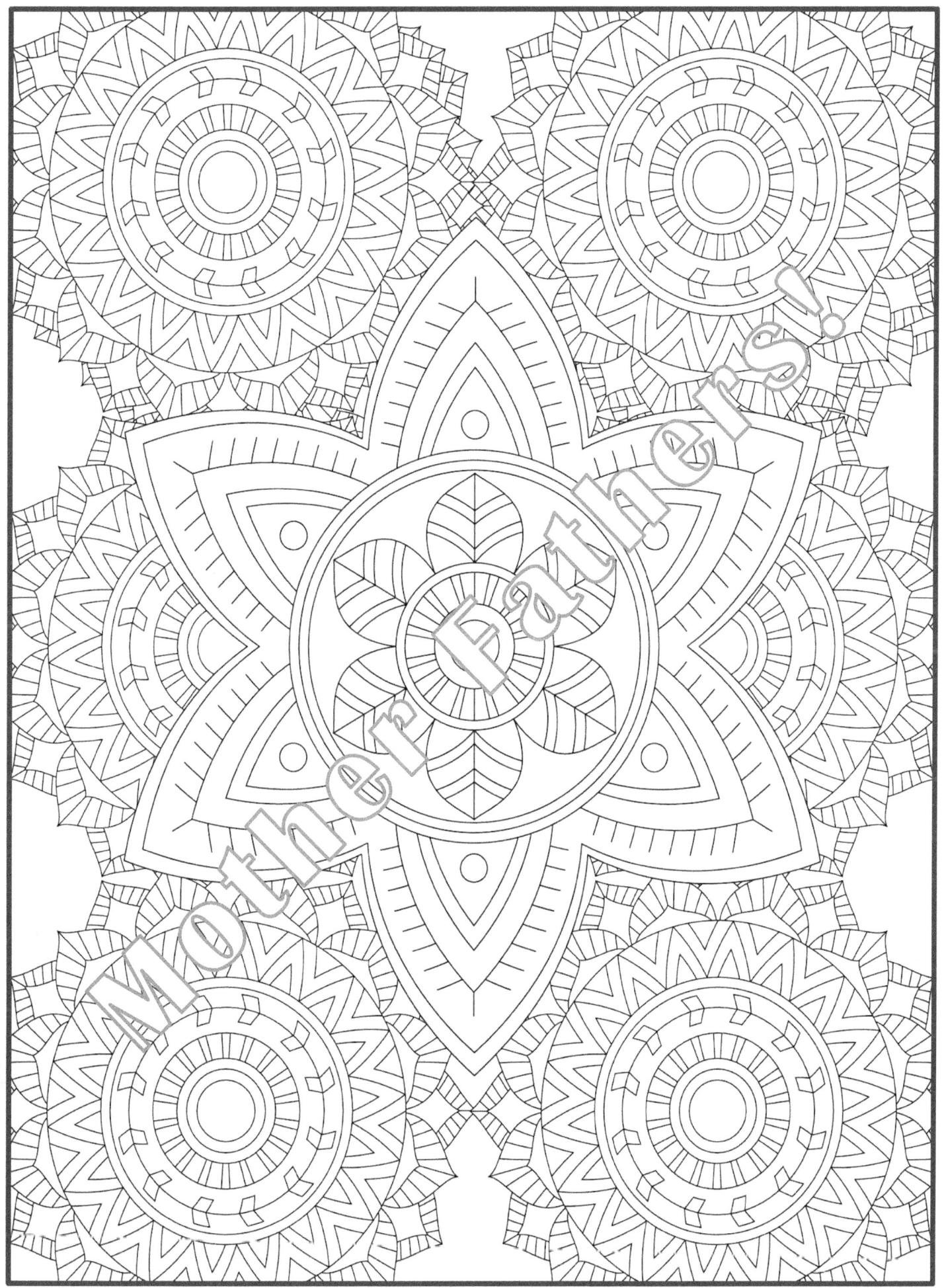

Page intentionally left blank for framing.

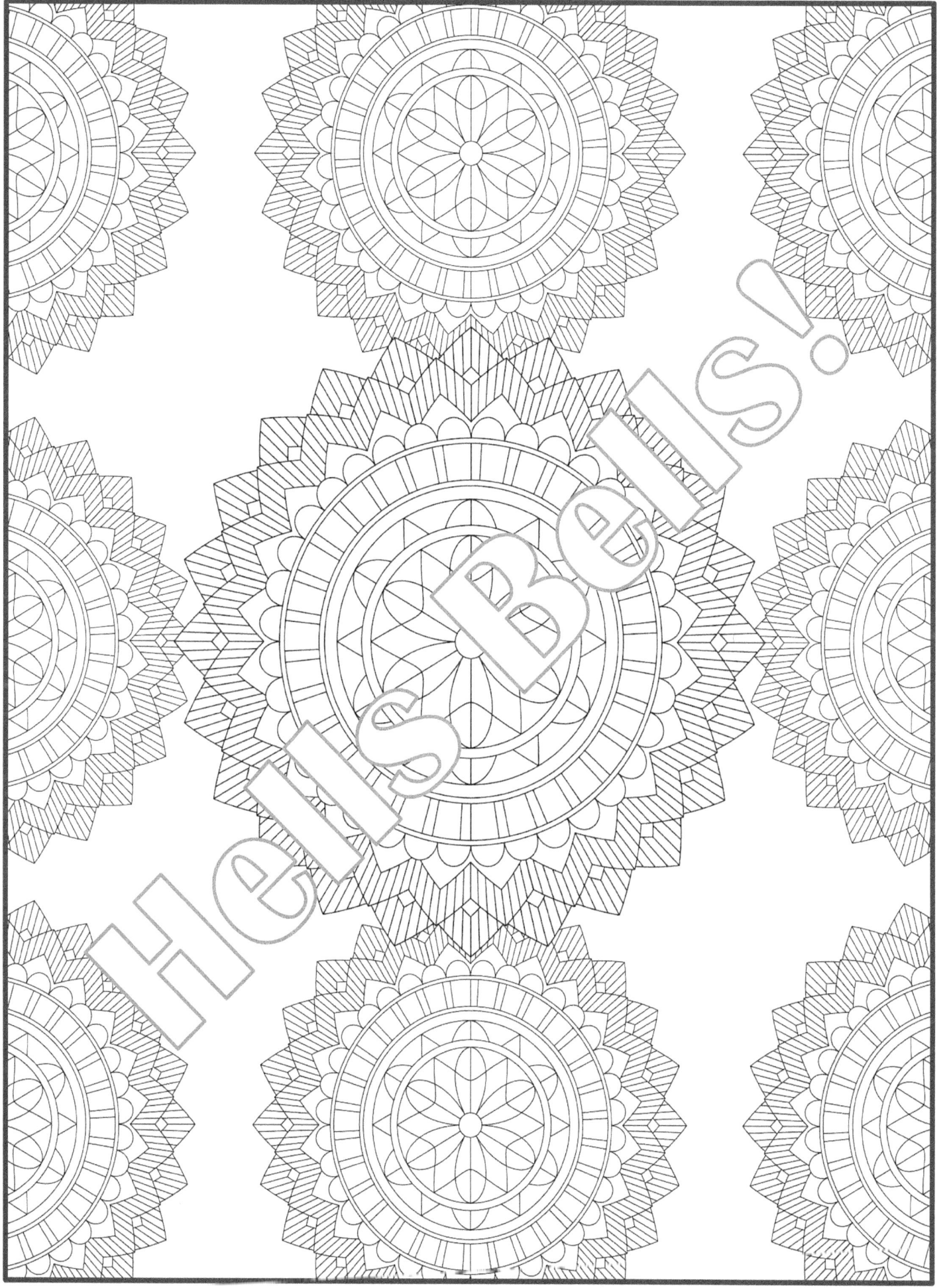

Page intentionally left blank for framing.

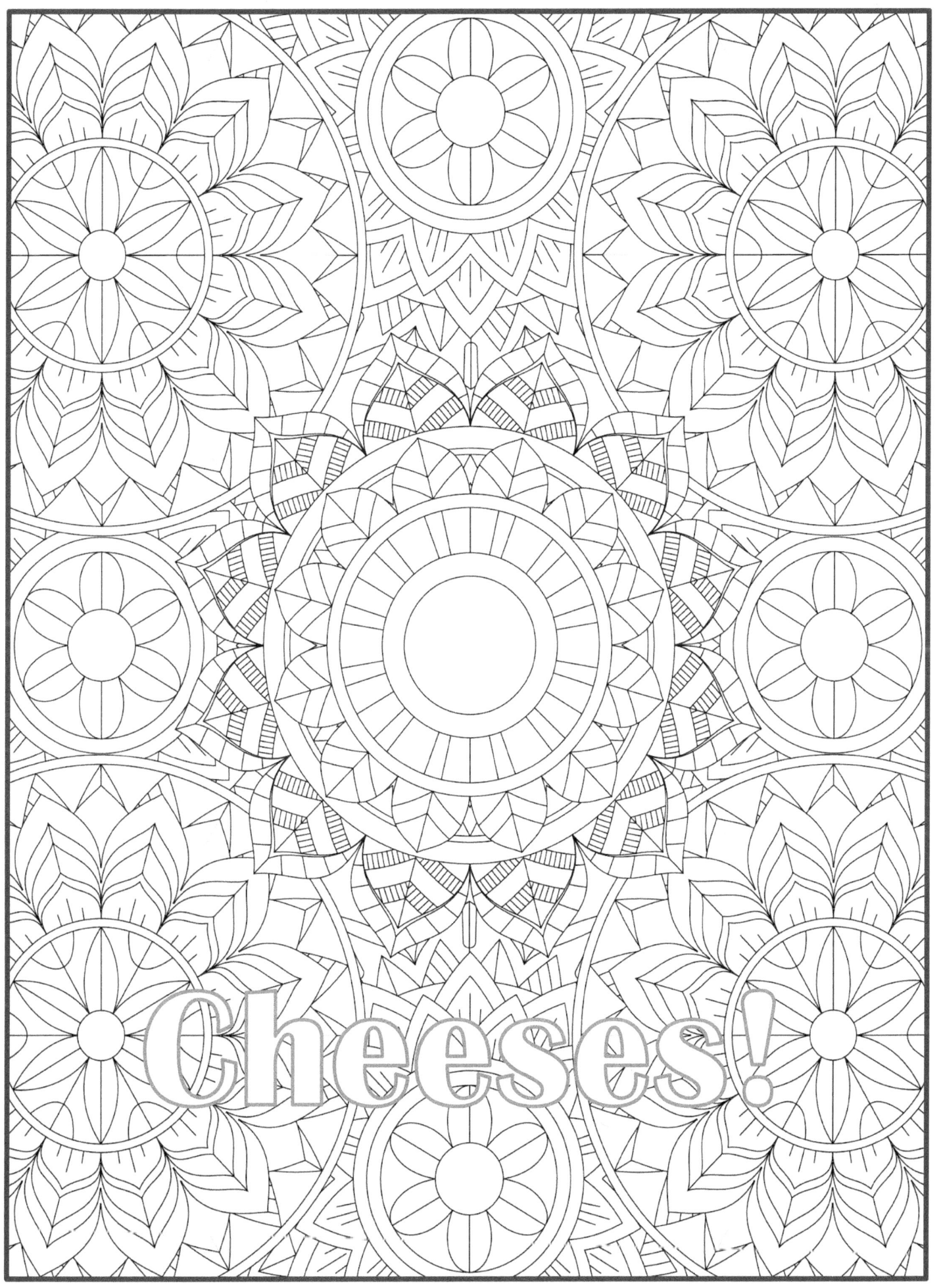

Page intentionally left blank for framing.

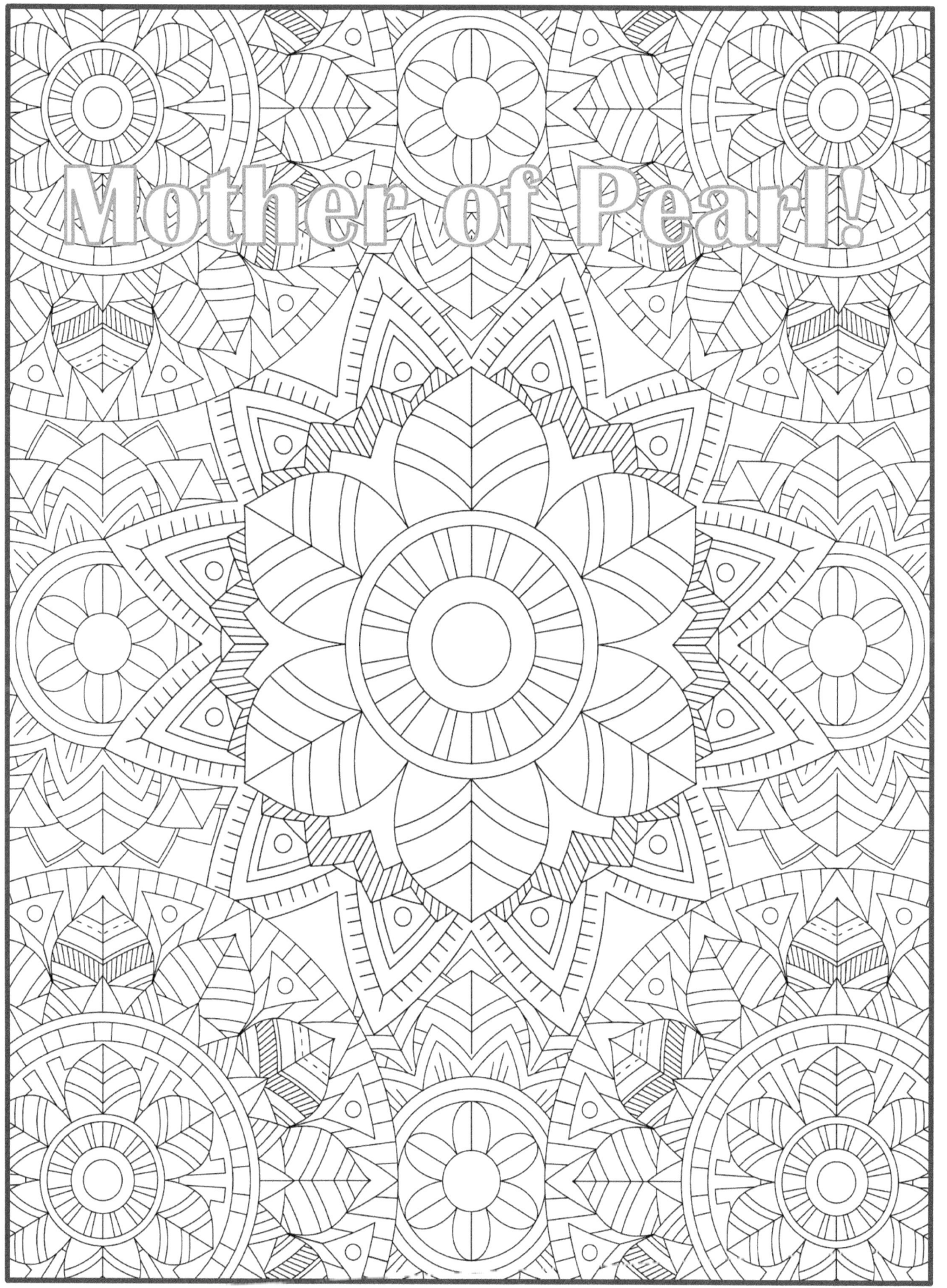

Page intentionally left blank for framing.

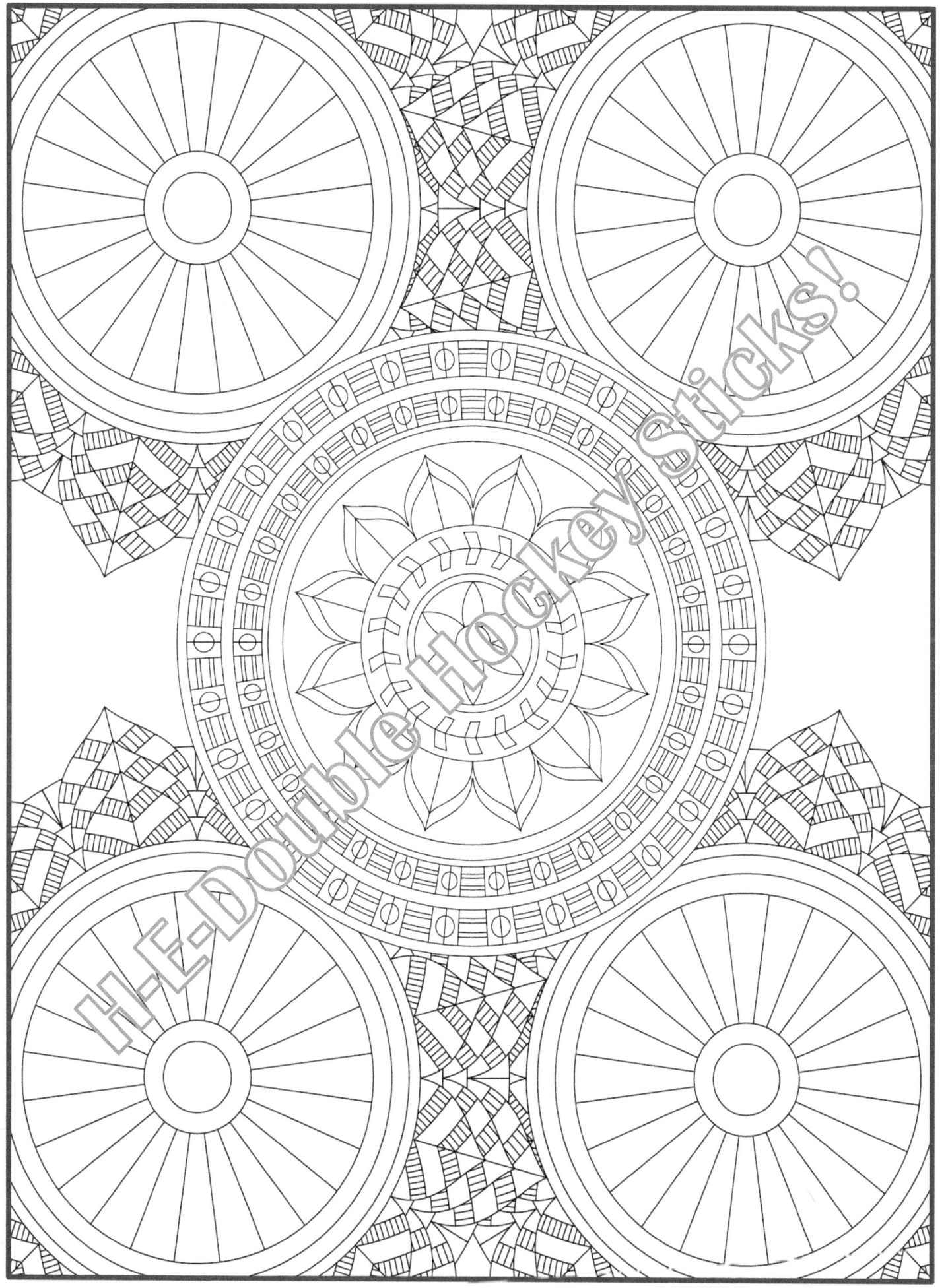

Page intentionally left blank for framing.

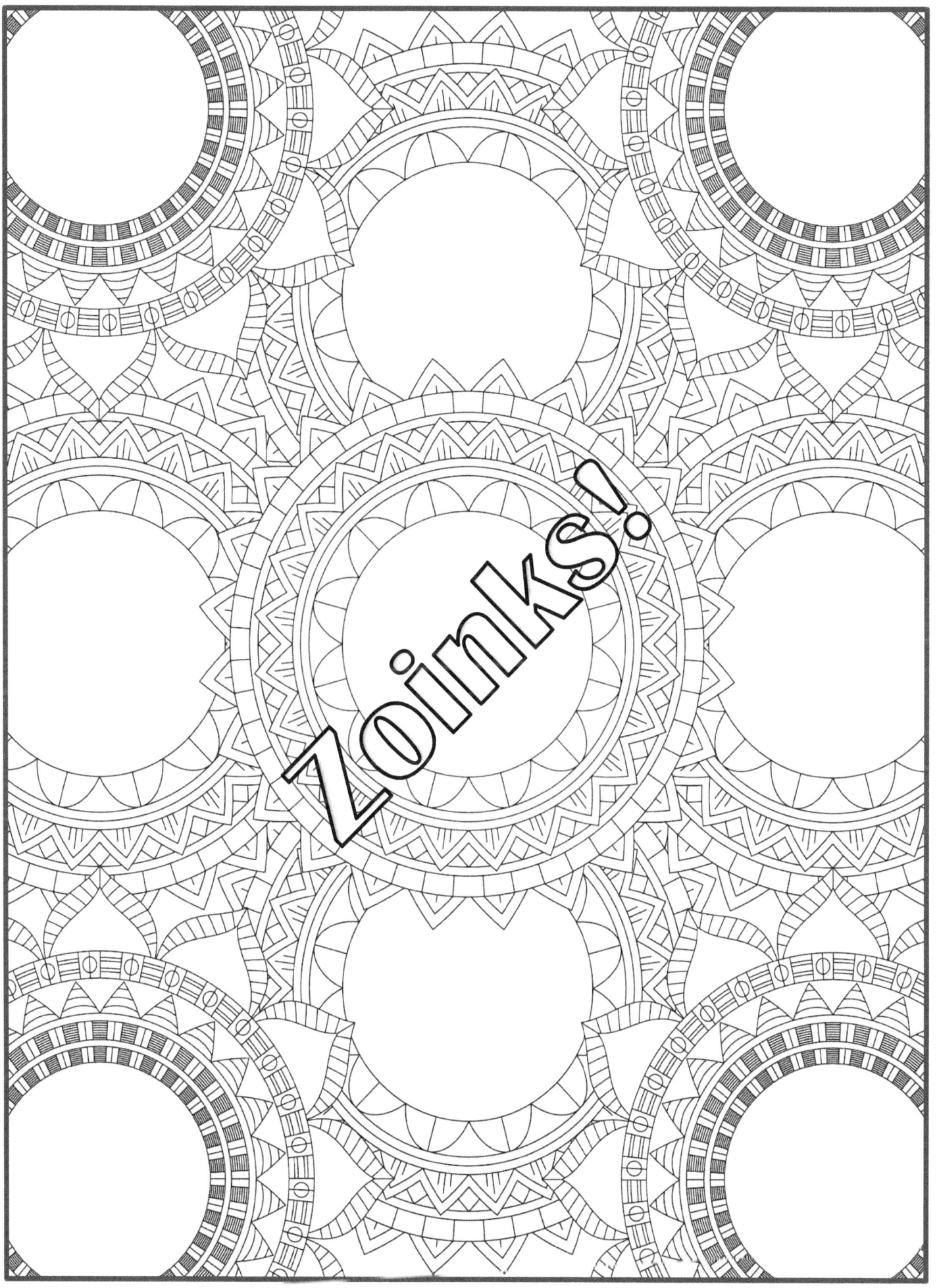

Page intentionally left blank for framing.

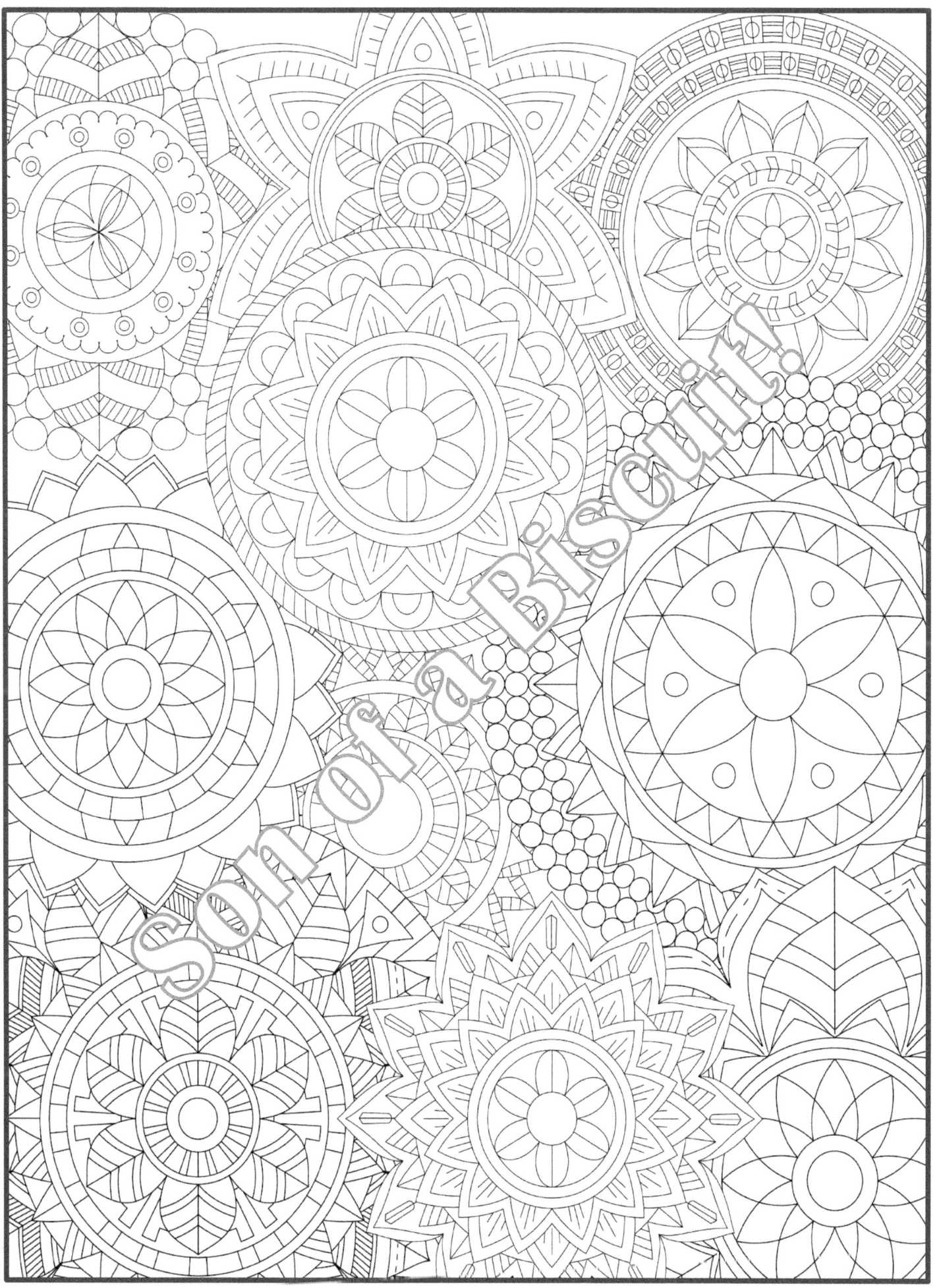

Page intentionally left blank for framing.

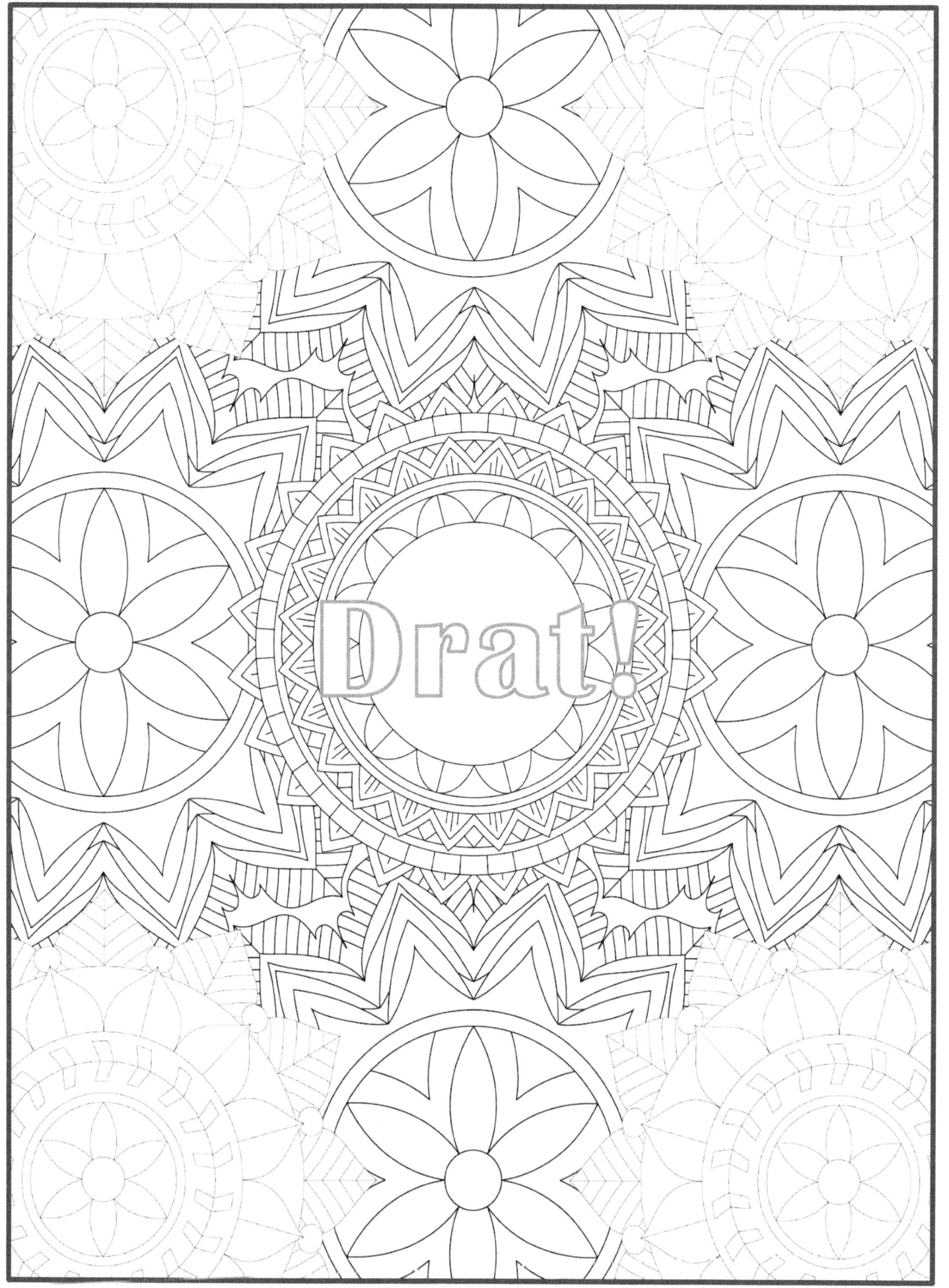

Page intentionally left blank for framing.

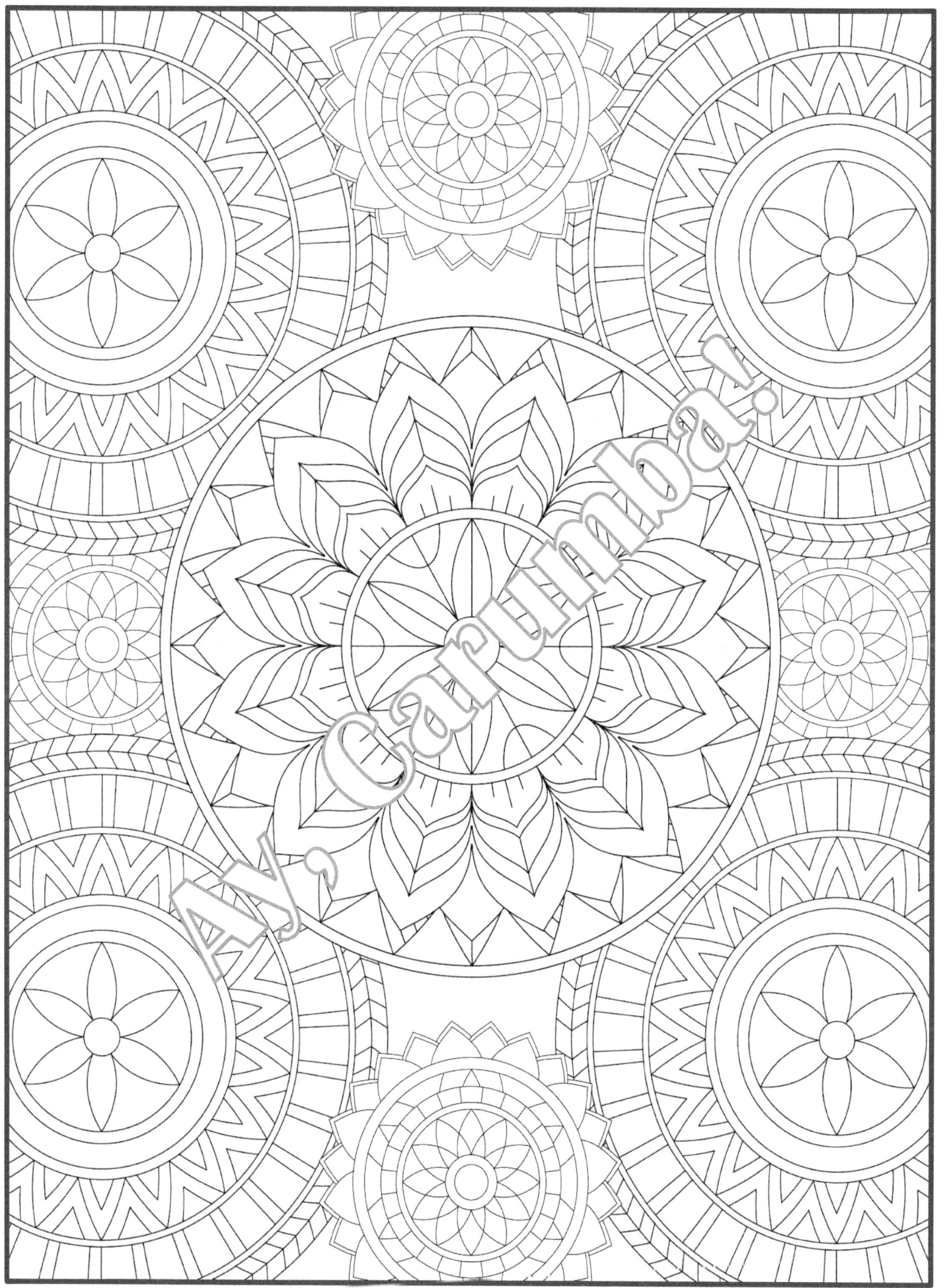

Page intentionally left blank for framing.

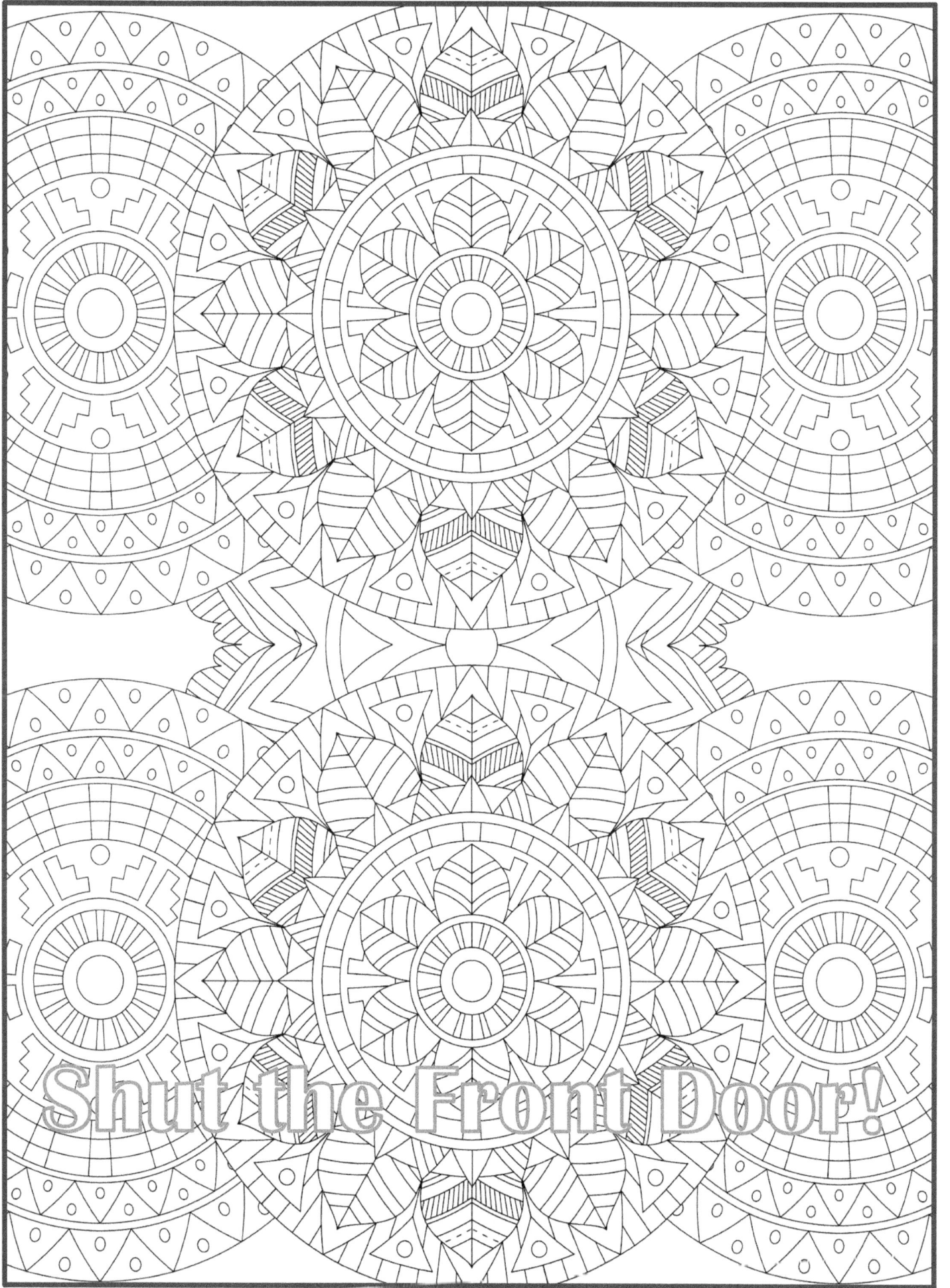

www.ingramcontent.com/pod-product-compliance
Lightning Source LLC
Chambersburg PA
CBHW081005220526
45467CB00008B/2704